"This Thing Called Poetry": An Anthology of Poems by Young Adults with Cancer

Edited by

Kathleen Henderson Staudt

Finishing Line Press
Georgetown, Kentucky

"This Thing Called Poetry": An Anthology of Poems by Young Adults with Cancer

Copyright © 2019
ISBN 978-1-63534-990-0 First Edition
All rights reserved under International and Pan-American Copyright Conventions.
No part of this book may be reproduced in any manner whatsoever without written
permission from the publisher, except in the case of brief quotations embodied in critical
articles and reviews.

Publisher: Leah Maines

FLP Editor: Christen Kincaid

Cover Art: Greg Staley

> *Wordfall: Currents* by Francie Hester and Lisa Hill is installed at the
> Teen and Young Adult Program Lounge in the Pediatric Center of
> Memorial Sloan Kettering (MSK), 1275 York Avenue at 67th Street.
> The piece draws on the poetry of Brendan Ogg, a 20 year old cancer
> patient who turned to poetry and art during his 14 month battle with
> the disease. The young adults undergoing treatment at MSK wrapped
> fragments of Brendan's poetry around 30,000 paperclips and in the
> process a community with a shared artistic goal emerged. Patients write
> their own poetry, engaging with the installation, which speaks to the
> power of words as legacy. MSK's new Teen and Young Adult Lounge is
> one of just a handful of programs across the country focused on this
> unique age group.

Cover Design: Elizabeth Maines McCleavy

Printed in the USA on acid-free paper.
Order online: www.finishinglinepress.com
             also available on amazon.com

Author inquiries and mail orders:
Finishing Line Press
P. O. Box 1626
Georgetown, Kentucky 40324
U. S. A.

Table of Contents

Sponsored by the Brendan Ogg Memorial Fund

Introduction

The title of this volume, like the project itself, is drawn from the poetry of Brendan Ogg, whose collection of poems, *Summer Becomes Absurd*, I had the privilege of editing in 2010. From his diagnosis at 19 to his death 14 months later, Brendan experienced much of what we have come to learn is a typical journey of a young adult with cancer: facing mortality when those around you believe themselves to be invincible and are at the peak of health; having no time for cancer in the midst of finding independence and love as well as juggling the demands of school, work, and/or raising a family. A gifted poet, Brendan navigated this time of life through his poetic practice, celebrating "how this thing called poetry can make a man feel free!"

Gathering the poems for this anthology, I have been recalling a conversation with Brendan early in 2009, at the Kefa Café—a favorite spot in downtown Silver Spring, Maryland. I had made a date for coffee with his mom, my good friend Jackie Ogg. According to his mom, Brendan heard about our planned meeting and asked to tag along. He had been diagnosed in December 2008 with brain cancer, and at the time of this conversation he was coming off of a grueling series of surgeries. He was wearing a backward baseball cap and walking with a cane, but I remember feeling impressed by how fully alive he was, for such a young person and given what he had gone through. He wanted to talk about poetry, and so we did: a long and lively conversation about Keats, and T.S. Eliot, about Brendan's work in poetry as a college student and especially about a recent poetry workshop at the Smith Center for Healing and the Arts, which had helped him to find his voice in a fresh way.

Brendan sought out this conversation because of something he knew we had in common: we were both poets, and he knew from the lore of our babysitting co-op that I had been diagnosed with breast cancer at 37, when my children were very young, and that I had started writing poetry out of that experience. The meeting between us reflected the cohort of poets who have been invited to contribute to this anthology.

The poems in this volume reflect the challenges that come with encountering cancer as a young adult, from anger to dark humor, from despair to a deepened appreciation of life and relationships. Some of the poets represented here are previously published, even well established, and we have included some work that is published posthumously. Others are relatively new to poetry, finding in it a medium for exploring and naming their particular experiences of life. Our hope is that the work collected here will give a fresh and compelling hearing to those experiences, for family members, caregivers and medical professionals, and that it may encourage other young adults to name and claim their own experiences as they continue with their lives, in the face of a cancer diagnosis.

Kathleen H Staudt,
Bethesda, Maryland, 2019

Interminable
Veronica Morgan

Just because I'm young doesn't mean they caught my cancer early
Doesn't mean the toxic remedies were tolerable
Doesn't mean I'm cured until I die from something else

Just because I completed active treatment years ago
Doesn't mean side effects do not persist
Doesn't mean I'm whole

Just because I've cobbled together a joyful life
Doesn't mean I don't grieve the loss of invincibility
Doesn't mean I don't bear the burden of reminders
Doesn't mean I can ignore the scars

Just because I made it to my son's graduation
doesn't mean I don't crave more milestones

Just because I have survived this long
Doesn't mean it's all behind me
Doesn't mean that I'll stop wondering

Will any of this
ever become
Inconsequential?

Just because my cancer was not terminal
Doesn't mean it does not remain
Interminable.

Cat With a C

Barlow Adams

When the doctors asked if cancer ran in my family, I told them it didn't, it stalked, pad-footed and quiet, leaving paw prints in blood along the widowed peaks of our high foreheads. I told them that the Big C might as well stand for big cat in regards to my family. That it did not speed through us, did not canter, that it perched like a leopard in our ancestral tree and watched with its carnivorous need, its Cheshire grin. I told them how it had stalked and hunted us almost to extinction, like a barn cat eradicating mice.

I told them how it came for my dad like a tiger, stepping out from the tall grasses of his double helixed DNA, bright and burning on the X-rays. How it settled on his lungs, sat on his chest and stole his breath like a baby's, purring its contagion into his esophagus until he couldn't talk, couldn't eat, until he drank his meals through a straw in his stomach and his skin hung from him like ancient wallpaper. Still it played its games, battered him for two years and when it finally closed its jaws we rejoiced and praised it for its mercy.

I told them about grandma, how her lips, boiled by snuff, looked like she lost her mouth pieces at a time, stolen away as if by some panther in the night. Each morning we'd wake up and she'd lost another nibble. Eventually it got her tongue, a bit of her chin. She sat in her rocking chair, being eaten alive, the cancer tearing out her windpipe with its slow, cautious claws. When we laid her in the ground, her casket closed tight to hide the hole in her face, mama tried to jump in the grave with her, and when they pulled her out, the oak bore scratches from her nails.

So when the doctors told me what lurked hidden in my T-cells, lymphocytes with teeth and talons, I told them I already knew, that I'd heard it screeching in my ears like a mountain lion since the day mama herself died of lung cancer, since they cut off my sister's breasts, since they found the lesions in my uncle's brain. I told them I knew the devil cat waited for me in the dark of my organs, under the cover of my skin, and that I was unafraid. See, I told them, I'd been waiting too, watching it for years, and I knew each and every way to skin that cat.

Collagen Matrix
Jodi Andrews

Skin emerged from skin to grasp; skin
to skin, my heartbeat moved on the waves
of the warm world's chest. My limbs outgrew

my skin, leaving stretch marks along thighs, hips.
My skin feels textured whispers: cotton, silk,
leather, dog fur, lotion, feathery flour. I feel kisses

on my cheeks, forehead, lips, my husband's
scruffy face, the nape of his neck. Behind
my knee, skin cells formed melanoma.

The plastic surgeon sewed fifty-eight stitches,
called it a "pivot," and marked me forever.
The scar only lays right when my leg's straight;

the shifted patch of skin is foreign land when I sit
and ride a bike and sleep with my legs scrunched.
I always hated certain textures like scratchy

turtlenecks, tights, a sweatshirt under my winter
coat bunching in my armpit. When I was young
and my parents drove me to school in snow pants,

I yelled and kicked. I hate the feel of denim on legs;
I refuse to wear my swimsuit on the drive
to water. Then, my scarred skin turned prison.

This basket weave stretched to let me stand again;
usually crisscross collagen lays parallel
to the skin's plane, but fibroblasts transformed

my matrix then rested, leaving skin pink, hairless,
numb. The etched P spells possibility, potential, poetry
—alive—everything my skin can feel, a melody.

After Radiation

Jennifer Franklin

The intensity of this joy
won't last. But it should.
I fear it's as fragile as robins' eggs

sheltered in that flimsy nest
last spring. I float home
with my spoils—a phalaenopsis orchid,

seven fuchsia blooms
wrapped in purple tissue
paper and a clean MRI report

in my plum purse, cutting
through mild October air.
As early as tomorrow afternoon

my gratitude will diminish.
I try to memorize this shade of sky,
the busker's hoarse voice

as he strums his broken guitar
on the subway stairs,
the cinnamon apple cake

the baker gives me when he kisses
my folded hands. The Wheaten
terrier's fur as I bend to him.

I echo Blake's etching—*I want,
I want.* Still human, I will never feel
this grateful again.

Counting
Katelyn O'Malley

She is told she is stage three, she is twenty-four
"it's the good cancer," they say
"don't worry, you'll be fine."
She starts to count treatments, close calls, missed opportunities
and then it's over and they celebrate
they take pictures and say, "Thank God" and
"you're an inspiration," and she starts believing it.

And then her scans come back.
She doesn't count anymore because
she would be counting years and odds and failed attempts
and she's no inspiration
she hasn't found meaning in this, she hasn't found purpose
or peace
anger is all she has found.

"The good cancer, my ass," she thinks
as she succumbs to anesthesia with her legs splayed open
they get three good eggs
"that'll give you a good chance at a kid or two," they say
she is twenty-five, infertile, menopausal to boot
"it's so unfair," some say
but she knows it's just pure bad luck
one tiny mutation that her body missed for any number of reasons
she worked herself a little too hard
took care of herself a little too little.

She is one year in remission now
they say after five you can call it a cure
now the threat of relapse is her new cancer
she, and it, will endure
it will sit dormant, quiet, in the back of her mind
always with her.
For now though, she will just keep counting.

How to Talk to a Sick Woman
Anya Krugovoy Silver

Do not make me your nightmare.
Refrain from invoking me among
the *A,B,C's of your fear.*
(There's no cure, it's true. That's why
I'm so blue.)
I'm not your *it could be worse*
or proof of the smallness of your woes.
My bad luck is not your good luck.
(And by the way, fuck you.)
Your pity, though meant to be kind,
undoes me. I find it dreary.
Nor am I the Madonna of cancer,
your bow-arched Amazon. Make me your inspiration
if you like, but I don't deserve praise.
My days are as ordinary as yours.
And when I die, what will you do?
You'll have lost your light-strung Santos.
Cede me back my story.
My veins spout open, then close like magic.
I don't dread death more than you do.
Only I get to say I'm tragic.

Tuesday (Meadowcrest)
Kimberly Jae

Just call me Mary
Motherfucking
Poppins
I'mma fly on a cloud
Sing a nice diddy or 2
And make all your pities and worries disappear

See. . . I'm magic

I can make tall stacks of bills disappear in one check
I can be in 2 places at once
I gotta go get my babies real quick
Gotta cook dinner real quick
I gotta get make this money real quick
Still trying to get this doctorate quick

I am nurse, doctor, lawyer, accountant, partner but foremost
mother
I can solve all your problems
So no I really don't have time

This little ole cancer thing don't take away
from all I have to do today
I ain't got time to be weak
I gotta be strong for everybody else

I have to make sure
My kids are okay
My mom's okay
My friends are okay

Is the audience okay?
I don't have time to figure out if I'm okay

I am the Family Rock and rocks don't get cancer

Remember I'm magic

I inherited this throne from my father. . .
I inherited this gene from my father. . .
I don't have time to die like my father
I still have kids to raise
Dreams to live
I'm the glue that holds everything together

His legacy is a noose that is strangling
the bit of life left out of me

He was weak
He. Let. Cancer. **KILL.** Him.
He was weak
He left this pain for me to fix
He left this cancer for me to fix
And I can't fix this

My magic no longer works

My kids still need their momma
Like I still need my daddy

Have I already left this inheritance for one of them?

I can't be weak but I can't be strong either
But I am Mary Motherfucking Poppins
And I still have to make this tall stack of bills
disappear in one check.

The End of the Appointment
Kyle William McGinn

> *And you would walk that road*
> *blazing, some days not even afraid to die.*
> —Katrina Vandenberg, "Connemara"

When you get out
of the hospital,
step into gray
March. The long walk

from the oncology
suite (those cubbies,
too big chairs and
tubes) will hobble

you. Your feet—already
numb—will flake
off. Small bits
of toe and nail

discarded onto the side-
walk, like confetti after
a parade. Outside, the
chemotherapy center cannot

follow you. The ladies
who knit hats for us,
the grandmother on her seventh
cycle. Thank God that you are

the youngest here. Continue
walking until you feel your knees
nub into the concrete
—at least you've been spared

the indignity of children
and their eggshell heads
blinding in hospital light
—those bright tired smiles.

Technology and A New World
Crystal Payne

I

On my 58th visit

to the hospital, a nurse asks

does it hurt? As she pierces

a needle in my arm, its silver

fusing with my venom

II

The old man shuffles with a card
at the bus stop. He hopes
for a savior. To help
him navigate the new technology. How hard
it has become to get a simple bus
ticket to the next destination. I take
the card from his hand and
push it in the machine. It spits
out a white ticket and he smiles. We
board the bus together. At the next stop
the bus pulls off, another old man
fumbles, left behind.
Outsmarted by a new world.

III

Radiation

I lie on the machine

breast exposed, nipples

pointed at the ceiling. 58 tiles

on the ceiling I wonder

why everything is always white

Krrrrrrrr The machine screams

beeeeeeep

it turns and I remain the same

at one with the machine:

It screams again.

Why Chemo?
Lia Burnham

When, still in bandages

you drop chunks of hair in the sink

and your eyebrows fall out

and you look like an alien

when you can't eat

or sleep

and your nails turn blue

and some fall off

and the you that you used to be

stares out of

sunken eye sockets

and everyone purses their lips

in sympathy

and your wig sucks

and you know it

and you can't stand the poison

they say is curing you

when you are a stranger in

your own mirror

that's when

your baby, with her little hand

touches your head and says

"Mommy, I like your bald hair"

and you cry because

life is short maybe very short

and you are lucky

very lucky

To My Neurosurgeon
after a month in rehab, unforeseen
Brendan Ogg

No longer can I feel the riptide roar of death,
Where black water overwhelms, and pulls beneath,
filling my lungs with sand.

I watched the neurosurgeon take his final, skillful stand,
inhaling that strange glioma beast after it had wrecked
the delicate snowflake patterns in my brain.

But here I am, alive and writing of it still,
of how on my victorious return,
he had the grace to apologize,
and how as I left he gave me thanks,
and said, "You made my day."
When after all, he had made mine as well,
and the one before,
and all of those ahead.

Poem to My Litter
Max Ritvo

My genes are in mice, and not in the banal way
that Man's old genes are in the Beasts.

My doctors split my tumors up and scattered them
into the bones of twelve mice. We give

the mice poisons I might, in the future, want
for myself. We watch each mouse like a crystal ball.

I wish it was perfect, but sometimes the death we see
doesn't happen when we try it again in my body.

My tumors are old, older than mice can be.
They first grew in my flank, a decade ago.

Then they went to my lungs, and down my femurs,
and into the hives in my throat that hatch white cells.

The mice only have a tumor each, in the leg.
Their tumors have never grown up. Uprooted

and moved. Learned to sleep in any bed
the vast body turns down. Before the tumors can spread,

they bust open the legs of the mice. Who bleed to death.
Next time the doctors plan to cut off the legs

in the nick of time so the tumors will spread.
But I still have both my legs. To complicate things further,

mouse bodies fight off my tumors. We have to give
the mice *AIDS* so they'll harbor my genes.

I want my mice to be just like me. I don't have any children.
I named them all Max. First they were Max 1, Max 2,

but now they're all just Max. No playing favorites.
They don't know they're named, of course.

They're like children you've traumatized
and tortured so they won't let you visit.

I hope, Maxes, some good in you is of me.
Even my suffering is good, in part. Sure, I swell

with rage, fear—the stuff that makes you see your tail
as a bar on the cage. But then the feelings pass.

And since I do absolutely nothing (my pride, like my fur,
all gone) nothing happens to me. And if a whole lot

of nothing happens to you, Maxes, that's peace.
Which is what we want. Trust me.

What We Have

Jennifer Franklin

for Max Ritvo

Our minds that plague and comfort us
with truth. The way neither of us will forget

how it felt for surgeons' scars to turn white
as bone. Last summer, all autumn. Winter

waiting for each other. Night already too dark
to reveal blossoms—pink and white—hovering

above. Talk of time, aware of what might have been
always with what is. Our one day together—

what we wrote to each other before and after. We are
the littered circus ground after the tents are pulled

and packed, all the animals pressed into cages. Our dry
bodies brittle, as if just days before they did not boast

abandon. As if you were not the thin clairvoyant clown.
As if I were not the trapeze dancer, flamboyant and fooled.

Eat

Kyle McGinn

I

Assorted boxes: hundreds of tissues
and ginger chews. The backward way of appetite

during chemo (betrayal
in the esophagus. It comes back up).

Strange to miss
the physical nature of eating, cancer

staying my churning jaw, wet
lips—sacramental filling

of empty space. Instead, a dull
echo reverberating in my inner ear.

The suggestion and honoring of duty:
eat this and you may live.

II

4th of July and syncopated
pop of fireworks outside

the bedroom window. I lie
on my side, surgery incision

leaking longways while kids
shriek joyfully under falling ash.

Later, my father drives me
to our family physician.

They weigh me, tell me
that I've lost weight

—thirty pounds in a week
and my dad clenches

the hinge of his jaw, hard lines
while they talk about diet

restrictions and the way a body
might eat itself.

Cachexia

Max Ritvo

Today I woke up in my body
and wasn't that body anymore.

It's more like my dog—
for the most part obedient,
warming to me
when I slip it goldfish or toast,

but it sheds.
Can't get past a simple sit,
stay, turn over. House-trained, but not entirely.

This doesn't mean it's time to say goodbye.

I've realized the estrangement
is temporary, and for my own good:

My body's work to break the world
into bricks and sticks
has turned inward.

As all the doors in the world
grow heavy
a big white bed is being put up in my heart.

Off

Amy Reichbach

one breast gone
I am off
balance,
leading me to
lean in
too much
to you.

Scars

Kathleen Henderson Staudt

Little by little, I am leaving behind
Pieces of myself:

Two well-used placentas,
       One miscarried child,
A breast, where babies nuzzled,
       cut off, as soon as it began
To turn to poison.

And in the aftermath,
those good and fertile years
       Tied off, by choice,
Yet not unmourned.

Now all I know
       is that I can never know
              what will be next to go.

Dressing, in the mirror,
       I read my life:
A tracery of scars.

Touching You

Lori Lasseter Hamilton

i don't care how you slice it,

there's just no being comfortable
in the "Touching You" dressing room

i wear a blue silk robe

while another lady feels me up,
measuring me with tape

i lean forward, then lift up, jiggle and wiggle
and let fall

this heavy pendulum of a surviving right breast.
The left one gone, chopped up,

sliced and diced like chicken cubes on a Hibachi grill.

what am i, an exotic dancer in a strip show,
onstage on a stripper pole?
no.
i'm at the "Touching You" store

with chemo wigs and rubber boobs,
and silky bras outlined at the edges with lace.
She's showing me the proper way
to put my "girls" into play,

Now don't i like the way i look

with my brand new "girls"

One of whom weighs ten thousand pounds?

no, i look like a sweater girl from the 1950s,

i wish i could sling this over the shoulder boulder holder off,
throw it down onto my bed

and go around half-naked,
wearing a regular bra without a pocket.

i wish i had the guts

but then people would ask me
what the hell happened
to my body?

So here i stand at "Touching you"
Letting another lady show me
How to dress "the girls"

When Someone Saw the Jagged Scar Behind my Knee

Jodi Andrews

and asked "What Happened?"
I replied "I had a bad mole"
because cancer didn't taste good in my mouth.

I would joke that a mole—the animal—bit me,
or I'd had a rendezvous with a shark—
"That would be a better story," they'd laugh.

At Taco John's, fresh stitches,
I stood on crutches to show a friend.
"I just lost my appetite," he said.

A three-year-old asks, "How's your scar?"
"It's feeling good" I reply
She fingers the numb shape of it, a P.

In for a physical, the doctor imagines
removing the 58 stitches that formed the scar
and says "You could buy creams, undergo
procedures to reduce the harsh, pink lines."

A Macy's clerk helping me fit a skirt
calls it "gnarly." She means intense,
but I picture a knotted, twisted tree,
rotting from the inside, tangled up in itself.

saying no
Amy Reichbach

her closeness to death
has cost her the luxury
of her belief
that there would always be
enough

she no longer
drops careless moments
as though the resources
were endless

instead she goes out
into the world
gathers the pieces
her generous spirit has
spread thin

to reconstruct
her life

I miss my Before

Amy Reichbach

I want my body back
overweight, unbeautiful
unmarked.
I want to remember
what it's like to hurt
to swell, to break, to cough
without wondering
whether it's back.
I want to know again my spirit
my belief in forever,
my innocence
that got lost when she left
I want to
talk to my former self
of the chaos to come,
the strength I will need
to get to today.

The Curse of a Strong Back

Kimberly Jae

People say my back is as strong as a mule
Strong as a brick wall blocking out the heat of the summer and the frost of
winter
Strong like a Mack Truck
but never soft
Never gentle
I wish my back were dainty

Wished my arms weren't chiseled from the weight of everyone's burden

My curse is a strong back
Strong skin
My back has no room for my own sorrows
The weight is too heavy
This strength is my curse

I rip my skin into strips of bandages
Tissue away the grimace
Bandage my pride
Pretend my pain doesn't hurt as much
I must be Ebony woman super hero
I am a not allowed human emotion
So I lie
Wounds do not exist as human
Tissue away emotions
Skin is too expensive a bandage to cry upon
So I don't cry on it

I want allowance to acknowledge weakness
To share this burden
To not have to do this alone
To not be less Black woman because of it
To heave breaths and not worry of the sound carrying
I just don't want to be strong
Just this once while bandaged in ebony skin and woman
Not have the answers to everything
Realize the world did not come to end

Kiss shoulders that house my tears' water
Know it will still be okay

Waking Dream
Kathleen Henderson Staudt

At the end of a long hallway—
    Autumn sunlight, soaking
    tended plants, polished floors,
    simplicity and order
    a silence
        that sings…
I do not belong here
    But meals have been prepared for me
    And I am
        welcome.
I move down the corridor,
    Alone,
    To a door with a card,
    And on that card
        Someone
            has written
                my name.

The Light This Morning

Kyle William McGinn

The light this morning
fractures over the window pane
—casts shadows across the bed.
I make it every morning, tuck
corners and sides beneath the box spring,
as if that ritual might make me new.

Au bade

Brendan Ogg

This pale human weariness;
the sun rises along the backs of mountainsides
at the end of every moonless night

I have seen I have seen I have seen.

This shyness of my feet to walk
has never been so astute,
or so acute,
as when I am with you.

…Careening cloudless goes the sky

Oh and I and I and I.

Nocturne

Anya Krugovoy Silver

I want to attend to the evening:
to impress on memory these roses,
unruly pink climbers, dishevelled white,
the bee-strung, heavy-haired lavender
planted between bushes for eye's ease—
the endless rung of moment after moment,
of rose-breath and globes of wild onion.
So many years I lived without paying attention
It was all boys and makeup and pop charts.
Maybe I wasted the beauty around me
because it still gleamed in my round cheeks.
Maybe my thick and shining braids bound me.
Grace withdrew from my distracted gaze.
Now that I lament, it's easier to praise
a promise that won't word itself—
the bush of half-bloomed, ghost-streaked
red roses offering at each angle
withered petals alongside sumptuous ruffles.

How to love a survivor

Amy Reichbach

touch me, here
but not only here
and don't be hurt
  if I pull away
let me feel the pressure
of your fingers, of your
   tongue
on my newly healed skin
touch my scars
  but not only my scars
allow me the moment
to take in a breath
relieved that I can feel you
—in some places at least—
that my body is whole
—or wholly mine anyway—
and as we make love please
let me experience
the depth of my loss
and the breadth of my found

Question and Answer: A Prophecy
Kathleen Henderson Staudt

        for Dana

"At the Resurrection,
will I have
two breasts,
or one?"

Oh, my dear—

At the Resurrection,
you
will be
beautiful.

To the Conductor Who Thought I Died Because I Now Take a Later Train

Jennifer Franklin

I didn't know I had worried you.
Or even that you'd remember me

after my treatment prevented me
from taking the train for months.

When you saw me again, I realized
you assumed my cancer had returned—

plucked me from your route
with the brutal force Hades used

to pull Persephone picking wildflowers.
You looked at me as if I had returned

from the dead. When you last saw me,
bandages lined my scared neck as if

they were all that held me together.
You couldn't know what keeps me whole.

That I still wake each day to kneel
on the cold ground that has not yet opened.

Afternoon

Max Ritvo

When I was about to die
my body lit up
like when I leave my house
without my wallet

What am I missing? I ask,
patting my chest
pocket.

And I am missing everything living
that won't come with me
into this sunny afternoon

—my body lights up for life
like all the wishes being granted in a fountain
at the same instant—
all the coins burning the fountain dry—

and I give my breath
to a small, bird-shaped pipe.

In the distance, behind several voices
haggling, I hear a sound like heads
clicking together. Like a game of pool
played with people by machines.

The first time I realized I might not be alive
Camila Saavedra

It bloomed on my skin the way kisses do when they land on your neck.

We had sat on the couch, music on, tangled legs platonic, loved,
short breaths keeping time while we reached over, swallowing
each other's exhales. Is it like this? As simple as just walking out
the door, down the stairs, staring at a balcony I'm not sure is even yours,
I can still hear you singing from all the way down here.

Four in the morning, I drag myself away.

I could tell you that my heart cried,
But I was tired.
Smoke and liquor sank into my tongue.
I drowned in it.

Goodbye October
Marika Warden (November 2010)

There's a rustle in the bushes

Not a cloud up in the sky.
I'm just watching trees change colors
And pretending they won't die.
So I'll take as many photos
As these canisters can hold
'Cause I feel like I've been dying,
I'm not even growing old.

Turning pages through my story

Running smoothly 'round the bend
I've outwitted every obstacle,
But every story ends.
Now I'm sitting on the terrace
Looking up at eyes of blue
And nothing really matters,
Not while I am here with you.

Goodbye October.

Goodbye to pastures lush and green
'Til the springtime winds of April
Blow away this winter dream.
Goodbye October.
Goodbye my wide-eyed rambling man.

Tell your stories to the wind
And I'll be with you once again.

Goodbye October.

In a year you'll reappear
But forgive me if my story ends
And I'm no longer here.
Goodbye October.

Let these memories stay true
And one day across the sea
I hope that I can be with you.

To Walk Away in the Nighttime
Morrow Toomey

Listen.

My eyes are a warning.

Silence.

The moon has changed shades of white.

A sprinkler to my right spits water on cement.

And I want to know if they know

The hours

I am hollow.

Like the inside of a tree filled with ants.

Like the insides of ants filled with tree.

My mind weighs a lot.

But it bleeds in muted colors

The sky cannot see.

And I won't speak.

Exactly Wrong
Brendan Ogg

I've played the game of love exactly wrong,
given a catalog of compliments with my first breath,
called at all the times when she was busy,
forgotten to posture as aloof,
dressed wrong, was ill mannered, etcetera.
I was prepared to hang my head and walk away—
but she, bright, smiling, draped an arm over my leg
as if I were more than the sum of all my actions
through the universe
that brought me to this moment,
where we wait, on a staircase,
glancing every now and then upstairs.

After All

Andrea Hackbarth

it comes to crisis
        every Sunday afternoon.

Maple syrup dries in spots
          on the counter.

A fourth cup of coffee is too much
but three was not enough
             to keep it all in place
balanced
       before the precipice.

If God was awake,
he was hiding   and
Om Shanti Shanti

just another empty hymn
fooling us
       with unfamiliar sounds.

Someone ought to wipe the counter
       or we'll get ants.

It's better not to watch

as we tumble
       off into morning

Talk About Something Else
Katelyn O'Malley

We sit in the far corner of a quiet café
and casually talk about dying.

We do this sometimes
we talk not about growing old together
and passing in our sleep, intertwined like the roots of an old tree
but about dying early, with a life unfinished.

We don't always get very far before changing the subject
because these things are hard to say
we don't know we are martyrs
but we're each preparing the other for the inevitability
of something that may not come.

In his thirties, he wakes each day
certain he is one day closer to succumbing to his mother's fate
one day closer to a slow, lonely descent into oblivion
and I, an even younger woman
live a life of disease, turning off and on like a switch.
Mortality has a firm grip and we are both trapped in it.

We sit here, we drink our cappuccinos
we watch the people walk past
we talk about how we should have kids soon
ready or not
so that they'll be old enough to care for each other
when Daddy loses his mind
and Mom eventually surrenders
or maybe we should spare them the trouble, and not have them at all.

We try to keep it light
saying all of this in lukewarm mockery
we know each other too well though
we both know the other isn't joking
so, we take a sip and we talk about something else.

Late Summer

Anya Krugovoy Silver

August evening, church bells,
light shattered on the quick
creek as in a Seurat painting,
grass thick with Queen Anne's lace,
the summer sun still so late
in setting that bedtime comes late
to the children scattered in the garden.
Late summer, and the roses in second
bloom know what's coming.
But for now, bells, water, laughter,
my mother and I walking together
arm in arm, because happiness
is a decision each of us has made,
without even discussing it.

Home
Brittney C. Block

We met in the Garden
Pardon me, but you're my neighbor
Your soft smile met my eyes
I blushed behind a glass of wine
You told me of your life, your job
and played a song I don't recall
I was busy falling
while my feet moved across the hardwood floor
and when you held me in your arms
I felt the voice of Otis Redding in my heart

South Carolina
Brendan Ogg

When we went to Carolina
I had come from thoughts of death to sight of life.
There was a taste to the water on my lips,
As if to confirm how far I'd come,
And how prepared I was to go the rest.
And then in celebration of this confirmation
I dove beneath a rolling wave and rode another to the shore.
On the shore I thought of Keats and wrote a poem to call my own.
How this thing called poetry can make a man feel free!

Water Women

Carole O'Toole

We arrive as strangers with our disparate paths
Our scars driving our destinies
Stretching our wounds
We turn toward the water
To cleanse us
To heal us
To bring us together

Quietly we steel ourselves
Lining up side by side
Focused and ready
Bending our backs to shoulder the weight
For each other
We move toward the water
To cleanse us
To heal us
To bring us together

In one swift movement
We slip into position
Eight voices strong and clear sound off
Shedding our skin, our energies merging
We enter the water
To cleanse us
To heal us
To bring us together

Arms cut
Thighs push
Hearts race
Steady and sure
The force of our wounded desires
Move us as one

With a single stroke
We are transformed

We are the water
Cleansing, healing, coming together

Contributors

Barlow Adams is the author of two novellas and an upcoming novel. His most recent publications include pieces at *formercactus*, Pine Mountain Sand and Gravel, *The Disappointed Housewife*, *The Molotov Cocktail*, *Ghost Parachute, Riggwelter Press,* and *Delphinium*. He celebrated his sixteenth year as a kidney transplant recipient this September, and has battled lymphoma for the last six. He is the luckiest man alive. He is 37.

• • • • • • • • • •

Jodi Andrews lives in Brookings, SD with her husband and baby daughter. She has had a melanoma, and two years later, a surgery to see if she had stage four melanoma. She did not; the enlarged lymph nodes were not cancerous, but she has written a lot of poetry about these experiences, including her debut chapbook titled *The Shadow of Death*. She now teaches English classes at South Dakota State University.

• • • • • • • • • •

Brittney C. Block is 29 years old. At the age of 26, Brittney was diagnosed with papillary thyroid cancer. Thanks to excellent doctors in Memphis, she has been cancer-free since June 2016. She currently works as a Regional Sales Execution Manager for the second largest broadcast company in the U.S. and holds a BA in Journalism (Advertising) and an MA in Journalism (Strategic Communications) from the University of Memphis. She volunteers with ThyCa Memphis, the American Cancer Society, the American Cancer Society Cancer Action Network, and West Cancer Center.

• • • • • • • • • •

Lia Burnham was diagnosed with breast cancer at 39. Her work has been published by *Every Day Fiction* and *101Fiction* and she has been honoured by Prose and The Angry Hourglass.

• • • • • • • • • •

Jennifer Franklin (AB Brown University, MFA Columbia University School of the Arts) is the author of two full-length collections, *Looming* (Elixir 2015) and *No Small Gift* (Four Way Books 2018). Her poetry has appeared widely in anthologies, literary magazines, and journals including *Blackbird, Boston Review, Gettysburg Review, Guernica, The Nation, New England Review, Paris Review,* "poem-a-day" on poets.org, *Poetry Daily, Prairie Schooner,* and *Verse Daily.* A selection of her poetry is featured in Andrew Solomon's National Book Critics Circle award-winning book, *Far from the Tree* (Scribner 2012). She is co-editor of Slapering Hol Press. She teaches poetry workshops and seminars at Bowery Poetry Club and Hudson Valley Writers Center, where she serves as Program Director. She lives in New York City.

· · · · · · · · · ·

Andrea L. Hackbarth lives in Palmer, Alaska, where she works as a writing tutor and piano technician. She holds a BA in English from Lawrence University and an MFA from the University of Alaska Anchorage. When she was 27, she was diagnosed with a rare form of non-Hodgkins Lymphoma, which was successfully "cured" with aggressive chemotherapy. Some of her work can be found in *Mezzo Cammin, The American Journal of Poetry, Southword,* and other print and online journals. She blogs about poetry and other poetic things at www.thelostintent.com.

· · · · · · · · · ·

Lori Lasseter Hamilton was 34 years old when she was diagnosed with stage 2 ductal carcinoma of the left breast. Lori had planned to be married in September 2004 to Robert, her boyfriend of 11 years who had proposed to her on Valentine's Day that year. But her OB/GYN doctor found a lump in her left breast during her yearly exam, so she and her fiancé decided to move up their wedding to date to May, before her mastectomy, chemotherapy, and radiation. She has been married for 15 years to her wonderful husband, who was by her side throughout her cancer treatments. Lori works as a medical records clerk at a hospital in her hometown of Birmingham, Alabama. She graduated from UAB in 1998 with a bachelor of arts in journalism. She has three poetry chapbooks: *"live, from the emergency room"*; *"sawdust, soap, soil, & stars"*; and *"body parts"*, which was published by New Dawn Unlimited in April 2018. Lori enjoys sharing her poems at open mikes in Birmingham, and she volunteers to help lead "Wordsmiths", a poetry workshop held once a month at her local public library.

· · · · · · · · · ·

Born in New Orleans and transplanted to Baltimore via Hurricane Katrina, **Kimberly Jae** is an actress, director, playwright, Slam poet, educator, mother and cancer survivor. K. began her career in the arts attending the famed New Orleans Center for the Creative Arts, and later received her BA, teacher and principal licenses as well as a Masters in Education. K. founded The PlayGround Children's Theatre Company in 1998 while still in college. Writing and directing children eventually morphed to teaching teachers how to teach children using theater and finally teaching and school administration. K. has served as a principal of K-8 charter schools as well as a teacher. Recently she opened a restaurant in York, PA. When not writing, K. slams and cooks whatever comes into her imagination. K. is the 2018 Pittsburgh Steel City Grand Slam Champion and the 2018 B.O.S.S. Queen of Steel Slam Champion. She recently won Steel City Individual World Poetry Slam (IWPS). Kimberly was ranked #29 in the world by Poetry Slam Inc. during the Individual World Poetry Slam. She has toured all over the East Coast and Ontario. Prior to her stroke, Jae was 2019 Steel City Poetry Slam Finalist, 2019 Guelph Poetry Slam Finalist and 2019 *Guelph Hot Damn! It's a Queer Slam* Guelph winner and was to represent Guelph at the Ontario province wide *Hot Damn! It's a Queer Slam* Finals. She is currently working on her first full length, *The Fuckery Monologues*, a sometimes tragic life story told in poems and photography.

· · · · · · · · · ·

Kyle William McGinn is a poet and labor activist. Diagnosed with cancer in 2014, he completed four rounds of chemotherapy and a major tumor removal surgery later that year. His poetry can be found in *Indicia, Typehouse, Poetry City, USA,* and in *Pennies*, a chapbook published by Red Bird Chapbooks. Kyle is a graduate of the University of Wisconsin - River Falls and recently received his MFA from Hamline University. He lives in Saint Paul, Minnesota with his wife, tiny dogs, and large cats.

• • • • • • • • • •

Veronica Morgan submitted a piece for this specific collection because she cares deeply about the young adult cancer community and related topics especially the long term impacts of treatment choices. Veronica is grateful to have such a long period of disease-free survival following her 2006 diagnosis of triple-negative breast cancer and BRCA1+, but has learned the hard way that the necessary radiation treatments, surgeries, and medications have consequences that never end. Veronica met and married a US Navy Chief after all her cancer treatments and surgeries. Dating after cancer was also a harrowing undertaking, but worth the risk to find love again. Veronica and Richard each have one adult son. At the time of the writing of this piece, Veronica was living at the sugar sand beach of Northwest Florida, but grew up in North Carolina. At the time of the publishing of this book, Veronica and Richard will be living in their tiny RV named Solar Gypsy while they undertake a post-military retirement adventure all over the US and Canada. Veronica enjoys reading, watercolor painting, art journaling, writing, and traveling.

• • • • • • • • • •

Brendan Ogg (1989-2010) grew up in Silver Spring, Maryland. He was majoring in English at the University of Michigan when he was diagnosed with a brain tumor during his sophomore year. He drew upon his lifelong love of reading and writing to deal with his illness. Top among Brendan's literary influences are John Keats, T.S. Eliot, Ernest Hemingway, and F. Scott Fitzgerald. Glad to know that his poems would be published, he was working on final revisions to his chapbook *Summer Becomes Absurd* just before he passed away on February 24, 2010.

• • • • • • • • • •

Katelyn O'Malley was diagnosed at twenty-four years old with Hodgkins Lymphoma. She received multiple different courses of treatments that culminated in an eventual stem cell transplant and a diagnosis of refractory disease. She participated in an immunotherapy clinical trial and finally found success with the course of treatment that came after the trial failed. Though her path was long and full of many obstacles, she was declared to be in her first remission in May 2016, after three years of continuous treatment. She struggled with depression throughout her journey and found peace and understanding in the catharsis that is writing. She is excited to see where life and writing takes her in the future.

· · · · · · · · · ·

Carole O'Toole is the Director of Integrative Oncology Navigation and Cancer Retreats at Smith Center for Healing and The Arts in Washington, DC. Diagnosed with advanced breast cancer at 38, her recovery from 18 months of aggressive chemotherapy, surgery, radiation and a bone marrow transplant was long and arduous. Since that time, she has authored two books on integrative cancer care, advised hospitals on integrative cancer services, and provided individual navigation services to hundreds of cancer survivors.

· · · · · · · · · ·

Crystal Payne was diagnosed with stage 3 breast cancer in 2016 at the age of 26. While undergoing chemotherapy, radiation therapy, and hormone therapy, Crystal worked toward her MA in English, which she recently completed at CUNY-Brooklyn College in May 2018. Her poetry and short stories have been published in the *Edisto River Review,* her articles published in *The Panther* Newspaper and *The Tatler* Newsletter, and her play, *Classic Man*, has been featured at the Atlanta Black Theatre Festival in November 2017. Crystal has won awards such as the South Carolina Broadcasters' Association Scholarship, the Rhetha M. Ford Award, and the Sigma Tau Delta Leadership Award.

· · · · · · · · · ·

Amy Reichbach is a Boston-based poet and public interest lawyer. A divorced Jewish lesbian mother who was diagnosed with breast cancer at the age of 38, she writes in themes of family, the Holocaust, sexuality, and illness. Living Beyond Breast Cancer's Writing the Journey and Lacuna Loft's Unspoken Ink, both online programs, helped her jumpstart her writing after her cancer diagnosis. Since then, Amy's poetry has been published by *Ink & Nebula* and *Montana Mouthful* and was included in Volume II of the *Hashtag: Queer Anthology*. Amy's advocacy work includes Living Beyond Breast Cancer's Young Advocate Program, Lacuna Loft's Young Adult Survivor Board, and One in Forty's Ambassador Program. She enjoys teaching, learning, and raising her daughter to be an activist. You can find Amy on Wordpress at turningreturningpoetry.wordpress.com and Twitter at @butIloveboobs.

· · · · · · · · · ·

Max Ritvo (1990-2006) wrote his poetry in New York and Los Angeles over the course of a long battle with cancer. He is the author of *Four Reincarnations*, published by Milkweed Press and his chapbook AEONS was chosen by Jean Valentine to receive the Poetry Society of America Chapbook Fellowship in 2014. Ritvo's poetry has appeared in the *New Yorker, Poetry,* and the *Boston Review*, and as a Poem-a-Day for poets.org. His prose and interviews have appeared in publications such as Lit Hub, *Huffington Post,* and the *Los Angeles Review of Books*.

· · · · · · · · · ·

Camila Saavedra is a poet and a cancer-defamer. She was diagnosed with Stage IV neuroendocrine pancreatic cancer in 2014, underwent surgery, and has had two recurrences. These recurrences led to chemo, radiation, ablation, more poetry, and a complicated sense of self. At 24, she finds herself again idling outside the boundaries of "tumor free." Currently, she is happily committed to the MFA program at Florida International University.

· · · · · · · · · ·

Anya Krugovoy Silver (1969-2018) described herself as "living and thriving with inflammatory breast cancer since 2004." We were grateful for Anya's enthusiastic and generous support of this anthology project and heartbroken to lose her in August 2018, just as we were going to press. Anya published four books of poetry, including *The Ninety-Third Name of God, I watched you Disappear*, and *From Nothing*. Her most recent book, *Second Bloom*, was published in 2017. Silver taught in the English Department at Mercer University. She was named 2015 Georgia Author of the Year in the poetry category and won a Guggenheim Fellowship for poetry in 2018. For more information, please visit: www.anyasilverpoet.com

· · · · · · · · · ·

Kathleen Henderson Staudt began writing poetry in her 40s, in the aftermath of a breast cancer diagnosis at age 37. She is a teacher, poet, spiritual director and independent scholar, and has worked at a number of institutions in the Washington, DC area, including the University of Maryland, Virginia Theological Seminary, Wesley seminary, and Washington National Cathedral. She has published three books of poems: *Annunciations: Poems out of Scripture*(2003), *Waving Back: Poems of Mothering Life* (2009) and *Good Places* (2017), as well as two books and numerous articles on the artist and poet David Jones. Kathy lives with her husband in Bethesda, Maryland.

· · · · · · · · · ·

Morrow Toomey is a recent graduate of Whitman College where she studied biology and fell in love with creative writing. Her work has appeared in Whitman's annual literary magazine Blue Moon. She is currently living in Anchorage, Alaska working towards a career in medicine. While she doesn't have the push of classes anymore to keep her writing, Morrow has a box of scribbled-on papers and a phone filled with notes on life's adventures.

· · · · · · · · · ·

Marika Warden is introduced by her Mom, Robin Botie as follows: Shortly after turning 18, Marika Joy Warden was diagnosed with cancer. And she did not want to talk. Not about cancer. Not to anyone. In addition to her disease she was fighting her doctors, her parents, the drugs, and anything that got in the way of living her life on her own terms. Her mother, in and out of hospitals with her for almost three years, chided Marika for being in denial, for not facing reality. Then, the day after she died, her mother discovered Marika had been writing about her life, her death, love, what it was like to have cancer and how it affected her relationships, ...the whole time.

Acknowledgements

We are delighted to share the work in this collection. We are deeply grateful to our friend Kathleen Staudt for her skillful editing of the anthology. Kathy embraced the project from the moment she heard the idea; sharing not only her time and talent but also her firsthand experience of cancer. Along the way we met other champions to whom we are indebted: Thomas Dooley, poet, teacher and bedside guide for young adults writing their way through illness. His generous and gracious spirit made the whole project something special; and Darlene Bookoff, poet, friend and supporter of the Smith Center for Healing and the Arts, helped winnow down the early submissions, injecting a sense of curiosity and deep respect for the healing impact of writing. Finally, to Finishing Line Press; thank you for celebrating the power of *this thing called poetry* every day and for offering the poets in this collection to chance to share their voice with others.

We are especially delighted to publish this anthology in honor of our son Brendan. Brendan loved to write and leaned into this gift as he dealt with cancer. While we knew his words would help form his legacy—and be a keepsake for us—we did not realize that they would also help us introduce him to so many others. We are honored to have him in the company of these talented contributors!

The Brendan Ogg Memorial Fund focuses on issues related to adolescents and young adults (AYA) with cancer. An estimated 70,000 young people between the ages of 15 and 39 are diagnosed with cancer each year—the AYA cohort, as defined by National Institutes of Health. This is 6-7 times the number of children aged 0-14 diagnosed with cancer and represents 5% of total cancer diagnoses in the United States. Navigating cancer includes addressing needs more pronounced for this age group: independence, identity, managing career and family, dating, fertility and friendships among others. The mind, body and spirit of a young adult cancer patient are different than a pediatric or elderly patient. Art and poetry offer many survivors some degree of spiritual solace and we offer this collection of poets and poetry as one way to glean additional insight into the AYA journey.

Jackie and Clay Ogg
Silver Spring, Maryland, 2018

Jodi Andrews, "When Someone Saw the Jagged Scar Behind my Knee" was published as an earlier draft in an issue of *Pasque Petals*.

Jennifer Franklin, "What We Have" appeared on line in The Scores and will appear in No Small Gift (Four Way Books, 2018). "After Radiation" will appear in No Small Gift (Four Way Books, 2018)

Brendan Ogg: "To My Neurosurgeon", "Aubade", "Exactly Wrong", "South Carolina", originally published in Finishing Line Press, *Summer Becomes Absurd*.

Max Ritvo, "Poem for My Litter" and "Afternoon" from Four Reincarnations. Copyright © 2016 by Max Ritvo. Reprinted with the permission of The Permissions Company, Inc. on behalf of Milkweed Editions, www.milkweed.org.

Kathleen Henderson Staudt, "Scars," "Waking Dream" and "Question and Answer" originally appeared in *Christianity and Literature* and were republished by Finishing Line Press in Kathy's collection *Waving Back*.

Anya Krugovoy Silver, "How to Talk to a Sick Woman," from Second Bloom: Poems. The Poiema Poetry Series. Ed. D.S. Martin. Eugene Oregon, Cascade Books, 2017.

CPSIA information can be obtained
at www.ICGtesting.com
Printed in the USA
FFHW020628090919
54793142-60481FF